WNBA
Records & Trivia

BY K. C. KELLEY

Assists superstar Courtney Vandersloot

The Child's World®
childsworld.com

Published by The Child's World®
1980 Lookout Drive • Mankato, MN 56003-1705
800-599-READ • www.childsworld.com

Photographs:
Cover: Elaine Thompson/AP.
AP Images: John Harrell 18. Newscom: Mingo
Nesmith/Icon SW 2; John Woike/Hartford Courant
9; Jeffrey Brown/Icon SW 9; Chuck Myers/MCT
10; Daniel Walker/SMI 12; Anthony Nesmith/Icon
SW 14; Nick Wosicka/Icon SW 16; Renee Jones
Schneider/Minnesota Star Tribune 21. Sports Team
History: 5.

ISBN 9781503835320
LCCN 2019944745

Printed in the United States of America

Contents

Super Stats!

The whole point of basketball is to score more points than the other team. That puts numbers and **statistics** ("stats") at the center of the sport. The WNBA's great teams and players have piled up tons of numbers. They score points and grab **rebounds**. They make **assists** and earn wins. Stats collect in games and in full seasons.

Get out your pencils and get ready for some numbers! This is a tour of the greatest stats and records in WNBA history!

Fans pack WNBA arenas like this one in Connecticut. They are ready to see big numbers on the scoreboard!

Pour in Points!

Without points, teams can't win championships. Some players have soared above the rest in scoring points. The WNBA's all-time points leader is Diana Taurasi. The Phoenix Mercury **guard** was the first to go over 8,500 **career** points. She averaged more than 20 points per game in seven seasons, too. Taurasi also holds the record for **free throws** made, with more than 2,000. Her scoring success helped her make 13 All-WNBA Teams!

◀ Taurasi set her records even though teams played tough defense against her.

Dishing Dimes

Dimes is a nickname for assists. Great passes are a big part of most scoring plays. Some players "dish dimes" better than others. The all-time WNBA leader in assists is Sue Bird. She was the first to reach 2,500 assists in a career. She has played her whole WNBA career with the Seattle Storm. Bird had a career-high 221 assists in 2003. Then she matched that in 2018!

Bird is about to let fly a perfect chest pass for another assist! ▶

Pound the Glass

Basketball **backboards** are not really made of glass. That would be too dangerous! They are clear plastic, though. That looks a lot like glass. The backboard's nickname is "the glass." Pounding the glass means grabbing rebounds. No one did that better in the WNBA than Rebekkah Brunson. At 6'2" (1.87 m), she was not the tallest player. She had a nose for the ball and pulled down more than 3,300 career "boards."

Brunson was an All-Star for the Sacramento Monarchs and Minnesota Lynx.

Stars from the Arc

Three-point baskets have been part of the WNBA since its first season. The long-range shots are taken outside an **arc** painted on the court. A big three-point basket can really change a game. A few players have been three-point stars. Diana Taurasi is the only player with more than 1,100 three-pointers. Katie Smith came close, with a total of 906 in her 15 WNBA seasons.

With the Minnesota Lynx and Detroit Shock, Smith made a total of seven All-Star teams. ▶

Single-Game Stars

The scoreboard lights up with numbers and stats at every game. Players can set several types of single-game records. In 2018, Liz Cambage of the Dallas Wings scored 53 points against the New York Liberty. That was the most ever in a WNBA game! She topped the 51 points that Riquna Williams had scored in a 2013 game. In a 2003 game, Chamique Holdsclaw grabbed a record 24 rebounds. How about assists? Ticha Penicheiro dished out 16 in a game . . . twice!

Cambage scored most of her points on shots close to the basket. She was traded to the Las Vegas Aces before the 2019 WNBA season.

Best Seasons

Stats add up over the course of each full WNBA season. For points, it's Diana Tarausi again! She holds the top two marks for most points in a season. She poured in 860 in 2006. She had 820 in 2008. Right behind her is the great Maya Moore's 812-point season in 2014. Sylvia Fowles pulled down 404 rebounds in 2018. That set a new WNBA single-season record. Courtney Vandersloot also set an all-time record in 2018. She passed out 258 assists.

Here's one more for Taurasi. In 2006, she made a WNBA-record 121 three-point shots. Katie Smith hit 246 free throws in 2001 to set a single-season record.

On the way to her record, Fowles had at least 10 rebounds in 24 out of 34 games.

Rookie Records

Starting out in a pro sports league is hard. You're the youngest player going up against older veterans. However, some rookies fit right in. Records can compare rookies from one season to the next. Tamika Catchings set the WNBA rookie scoring record in 2002. She scored 594 points for the Indiana Fever. That good start led to a great career. Catchings made 12 All-WNBA teams!

In her record-setting season, Catchings twice scored 32 points in a game.

All About the Ws

Every team wants to end the season with a trophy. Winning the WNBA title is hard work, though! Only two teams have earned four season championships. The Houston Comets won four in a row starting in 1997. That was the WNBA's first season! The Minnesota Lynx tied that record in 2017. The Lynx won their first title in 2011. In 2019, the Los Angeles Sparks became the first team to win 450 **regular-season** games.

Maya Moore was all smiles after she and her Lynx teammates won the 2017 WNBA championship. ▶

Glossary

arc (ARK) a curving line or path

assists (us-SISTS) passes that lead directly to baskets

backboards (BAK-bords) clear plastic panels to which the rim and basket are attached

career (kuh-REER) the length of a person's professional life

free throw (FREE THROW) a shot awarded following a foul, taken from a line that is 15 feet (4.5 m) from the basket

guard (GARDZ) a basketball position that often makes passes

rebounds (REE-bowndz) balls that bounce away after a shot is missed

regular-season (REG-you-ler SEE-zun) the scheduled part of a pro sports year before the postseason playoffs

statistics (stuh-TISS-tiks) numbers that record events

Find Out More

IN THE LIBRARY

Buckley, James Jr. *It's a Numbers Game: Basketball.* Washington, DC: National Geographic Kids, 2020.

Levit, Joe. *Basketball's G.O.A.T.: Michael Jordan, LeBron James, and More (Sports' Greatest of All Time).* New York, NY: Lerner Publishing, 2019.

Sports Illustrated Kids. *My First Book of Basketball.* New York, NY: Sports Illustrated Kids, 2018.

ON THE WEB

Visit our Web site for links about the WNBA:
childsworld.com/links

Note to Parents, Teachers, and Librarians:
We routinely verify our Web links to make sure they are safe
and active sites. So encourage your readers to check them out!

Index

About the Author

K.C. Kelley is the author of more than 50 books on sports for young readers, as well as many sports biographies. He lives in Santa Barbara, California.